# How Without A Dad

Tips And Stories From The Okayest Dad Around

## By Jose De La Roca

JoseDeLaRoca.com

While every precaution has been taken in the preparation of this book, the publisher assumes no responsibility for errors or omissions, or for damages resulting from the use of the information contained herein.

Copyright © 2018 by Jose De La Roca
All rights reserved. No part of this book may be reproduced, scanned,
or distributed in any printed or electronic form without permission.
First Edition: May 3rd, 2018
Printed in the United States of America

# TABLE OF CONTENT

Intro..................................................2
Rewrite The Past................................3
Love Wont Feed Your Family.................15
There's No Crying In Baseball, Only In Fatherhood..............................21
Papa Says, Pow Pow ............................25
I'm Not Asking You, I'm Telling You......30
105....................................................36
Growing Up With An Immigrant Parent................................................42
A, Not Plus......................................... 53
Booze & Childhood............................. 61
You Had a Male Role Model..................70
Life Is Short, Just like me.......................78
Tips & Tricks........................................85
Happy Fathers Day, You Get A Break!...91
From: Me, To: You................................93
About the Author..................................96

Intro

# HOW TO BE A DAD WITHOUT A DAD?

Simple, have unprotected sex and don't have a dad.

But, if you are planning to stick around for the ride and raise your incredible baby as I have with my amazing son, hopefully, my experiences through overwhelming struggles and extraordinary achievements can give you a helping hand to become the father that neither you nor I ever had.

So sit back, relax, enjoy and learn from all the mistakes I have done to become the okayest dad around.

## Chapter 1

# REWRITE THE PAST

I didn't want to have kids because I was afraid that I would become my dad and ruin that child life. I didn't want my child to suffer the way I did, and struggle the way I did. I didn't want my child to be me. So when my Girlfriend told me that she was pregnant, I almost fainted and ran over a couple of people at work.

At the time I was working as a train conductor at a mall. Yup, I gave rides to little kids on a trackless electric train. I was totally financially ready to be a great dad! It was a shock because my Girlfriend was not supposed to have kids. My Girlfriend had suffered from really bad menstrual pains, and when she was visiting her family in Mexico, she had an ultrasound done and discovered she had three tumors next to her uterus. She had them removed, and when she went back for her monthly checkup they discovered cysts on her ovaries and fibroids in her uterus. The doctor told her that her body produced those and it was common for an older woman but not women her age. That there was a possibility she would never have kids. When she told me that, I stopped using a condom. The doctor told her that her surgery would be properly healed in twelve months. Well, she got pregnant thirteen months after her surgery. She was in Mexico again visiting her family and did another ultrasound, and she discovered she was pregnant. She told me via text! I saw the text right before I gave a ride to a mom and her son on the train and I almost ran over a couple of people at the mall during that ride. I was going to faint so decided to take a break and breath. My first thought was never about getting an abortion or leaving her or not raising my child; my thought was that I needed to be better and improve my life. Better financially, mentally and physically. I needed to help myself, before I can help my Girlfriend and my son. It's not until now, that I see that right there in that moment I was better than my biological dad. I was not going to leave my child be fatherless. I was going to work hard to provide better things for him. I was going to get in better shape to last longer for him, I was going to be more focused to help him struggle through life, and lastly, I was going to be there all the way with him no matter what the circumstances were.

Up to that point, I didn't want to have kids, but after that, I couldn't wait to have him. I'm happy to be a dad. It's not easy at all being a father. It's very hard, but I don't care because from now on, my only job is to be a dad.

Was I ready to be a dad? Yes, but I would have wanted to be better financially. Before my son was born, I always said that I didn't want to have kids. Now that I look back, it was the right mentality to have because I wasn't ready to be a father. I was still enjoying life, drinking, partying and enjoying my freedom. When I got the news that I was going to be a dad I had already traveled the country, partied more than many have and definitely drank more than most have so I was ready to step aside from all that, and be a full time dad. I believe that in a perfect world no one should get marry or decide to have a child if they still have the "What If." It is a dangerous thing if you still have the "what if." What if I go to Italy, what if I have sex with a Brazilian girl or man, what if I get a mustang? To be able to settle and accept all the responsibilities as a parent, husband or wife you can't have the "what if". This doesn't mean you can't travel or get a mustang when you have kids. It means that if you didn't get the mustang when you were young and single, you are going to have to wait until your son is older or you are better financially to do it. It sounds simple, but it's not. Most marriages will fall apart because one of the partners still hasn't experienced enough and they still want to party, drink, experiment with drugs, have sex with different people, travel or buy crazy things. So if you are reading this and you are deciding whether to get marry or have kids ask yourself, do I still have the "What If"

Am I going to be the best dad? Probably not, but I won't stop trying. My whole adult life, people always told me I was going to be a great dad and that would get me mad because I hated my dad and I thought I would never have kids. It seemed like I was good with kids. Every time I went to a party I ended up playing with the kids or the dogs. When I would ride the bus all the kids would stare at me like if I was a giant monkey made out of chocolate. I do have the height of a twelve-year-old boy and act childish but how could kids and pets tell that? I always liked kids, they tell the truth, and they are fun. I guess I'm just a big kid that just got older in age. I was destined to have kids, but for now one is enough. I have to be responsible and not have a whole basketball team. If you are going to raise a great kid, you are going to need a lot of time and resources. I always get mad when I see a mother of three in the bus. She never had the right set of mind to realize that having more than one kid would diminish her financial status and diminish her time. When you have your first child, you have to make a plan and see if your financial status would allow you to give him a normal life. Can I afford one kid? If I have another kid, will I provide half of what I can provide to this one? Etc. So when I see the mom struggling with her three kids in the bus, I get mad at her and her family for not planning better for the future of her kids. Kids are expensive and the more kids you have, the less money and time you will have to give each one of them. So if you have one healthy child, think twice about having another one. Just think of your childhood, use your own experiences to decide what is best for your own child. What worked during your childhood and what did not. What benefitted you and what hurt you? Use that to become a better father. Did your parent ever say they couldn't afford this or that and why? Did your brother get better things than you did? Did you get better things and your siblings hated you? Time and money are essential keys to raising a kid, and I'm ready for the challenge. For now, I'm happy with only one.

My son's birth was quicker than most men use the restroom. When they removed my Girlfriend tumors next to her uterus, they did a surgery just like you would do a C-section birth, so my Girlfriend had to have a C-section birth. They said that once you had a C-section birth, you could only have C-section births from now on. They also say that you can only have three C sections surgeries. So technically my Girlfriend can only have two children. My son's birth was planned on a date and time. We arrived at the hospital around 7 pm, they set everything up, and my son was born around 9 pm. My Girlfriend was pregnant, and 10 min later my son was born, simple as that. Took 10 minutes from when we went in to the surgery room to the time my son was born. I'm never going to forget the sound when they open the placenta and my son was born and started crying. It's this Pop sound, like a water balloon being popped but fuller sounding. After the pop, I heard my son cry, and I saw my Girlfriend in tears. I was a dad! The best part besides my son being born was the anesthesiologist. I was told I could bring my phone with me, so I did. I wasn't planning on taking my phone out and taking pictures or video. But I brought my phone with me just in case. As soon as my son was born the anesthesiologist asked me why I wasn't taking pictures. He made me take my phone out, made me give it to him and told me to go see my son. Then he took pictures of my son and I while I cut my son's umbilical cord. Then I took my son and showed my son to my Girlfriend, and he made us take a couple of pictures with different poses. It was pretty funny and weird that this doctor was doing a photo-shoot right there during my son's birth. Thanks to him I have great pictures and memories that would last forever.

The recovery for both of them started right after my son's birth. Being there those 72 hours after her surgery made me admire women more. The pain and struggle that she suffered I don't think I would have handled it the way she did. They cut her right on her pelvis. Every movement of your body goes thru your pelvis. Try it. Put a hand on your pelvis and try to move, you'll feel that your pelvis moves. She had a 10-12 inch cut there. My son was healthy and in great shape, and we stayed in the hospital for about three days for her to recover. It was very painful for her and for me to watch. The nurses and doctor told me there was nothing I could do but support her and help her. Only time and movement would help her heal. If your Girlfriend or wife is pregnant, I hope she has a natural birth. A natural birth can be very painful for hours but after the baby is born is not as bad as a C-section surgery would be. The recovery of natural birth is very simple compare to a C-section. She had a catheter to help her pee and the nurses took very good care of her and the baby. Twenty-Four hours after my son was born they told her she had to get up and walk by herself. This wasn't pretty. They helped her get up and walk, and when she got up, they took the catheter out. This was one of the worse things I ever saw. The pain my Girlfriend experienced I have never seen it or wish upon anyone. I felt like grabbing the nurses and making them stop, but there was nothing I can do. They had explained to us that this was the only way she'll get better and had to be done. My Girlfriend's mom was there, and I had to grab her because she was ready to beat up the nurses. It was not a great experience, but she did it. She did it screaming and crying, and she walked and pee by herself. From then on I applaud her, and I know how strong and brave of a person she is. She is my rock. There was one thing I didn't like at all in our stay at the hospital, and if I ever have another child, I would do things differently. I would not have people visit after my son is born. No one would be allowed to visit us after my son is born. I would ban all of our families from visiting us. Maybe her mom can be with us to help us watch the baby while we sleep, but that's all. Anyone who wants to come and see the baby when he is born would be welcome. Stop by, take your picture and bye, see yah in a couple of weeks. We were at the hospital for about 3 days, and people came and went. They just wanted to see and touch the baby. Some of them never washed their hands. What made me most angry was that most of them didn't see that my Girlfriend was in a lot of pain and needed to rest. Only a couple of people actually cared about her well being, and only 2 people asked me how I was and if I needed anything. Do you want to be supportive and considerate? Don't come. While their presence may show support, it also required that my Girlfriend greeted them, made conversation and stayed awake as a courtesy. I can't be rude and not let you touch and carry my brand-new baby but be considerate. If he is asleep, don't wake him up and wash your hands before you touch him. It was more of a party than a time of healing and quiet. Most of the people who showed up are not part of our close family anyways. One of her aunts called me a coward after she asked me when was the other baby going to be born and I told her I didn't want another one. My son was just born, and this lady who I barely know calls me a coward because I know I can't afford another baby? She was lucky I love my Girlfriend, and I have tons of respect for my mother in law that I didn't kick her out of the room at the time. If you really analyze the situation, my Girlfriend was going through the worst pain possible and my son was in shock. All they needed was peace and rest. So I don't mind having twenty people show up the moment he is born and see him and take pictures through the glass, but I wouldn't have visits after that. Am I being selfish and impolite? Damn right! If you really see the big picture, I'm just looking out for the wellbeing of the two most important people at the time, my Girlfriend and Son and if you don't see it then be it. Those two days my Girlfriend needed to rest 24/7, and she didn't get to. My son didn't need to be touch and carry by everyone, and I didn't want more worries than I already had. So, my advice to you is not to have too many people around after your baby is born especially if your Girlfriend or wife is in recovery. Have one person closest to you if any and that's all.

Everything changes after you become a parent. I went from "move bitch, get out the way" to "the wheels on the bus go round and round." It's all about your child from now on. You become second in your own life. Every decision you make would be based on your child needs, schedule, and mood. If you are planning to take your baby to Coachella, maybe you want to re-think it. I know Beyoncé is going to be there but maybe you can leave your baby with your parents or just wait a couple of years to go see queen bee, she'll be around for a long time.

At this stage of my life, I have become a better dad than mine, and I hope to keep moving forward and improving. For what I heard my dad quit drinking when I was young and became a civil engineer. That's great for him and for what I heard he is a smart man. I hope he has good health and becomes a better man too. He wasn't part of my life, never supported me, never helped us or tried to be a dad. I forgave him a long time ago and wished him the best. I hope to always be a part of my son's life no matter the circumstances. I would always be a part of his life and will try to support him at all cost. At the end of the day, all we should strive to be is be better than our parents, and we should want our kids to be better than us.

Don't let your past determine who you are or will be. Analyze the past and learn from the mistakes you and others did. If your dad wasn't there for you, then you be there for your child, if your dad didn't say I love you, then you say I love you to your son, if no one taught you how to talk to girls, then you show your son how, and if no one went to your games, then you go to all your child games. Don't be your past or people from your past, be better.

Everything that you have done or not done in the past has molded you to be the father you are and will be. Get rid of your bad habits. Become a better person and ultimately a better dad.

You don't have to become your past; you can be better than your past. If your dad was not part of your life, or if your dad left your mom when you were little, and you decided to stay with your partner and raise your child you are better than your dad. If you decided to be responsible and take care of your baby even though you aren't together with the mom of your child, well, you are better than your dad who left you. I know I am.

**PS**. I always tell people I got tricked to be a dad.

Chapter 2

# LOVE WON'T FEED YOUR FAMILY

Most people of my generation either grew up with no father or their father was old school and didn't say I love you much. An old school dad would have a full time job that he hated and would bring home the paycheck to the mom for her to pay bills and buy food. He would work hard to provide for his family because that's what a man supposed to do. Most likely that same dad didn't spend too much time with his kids. He would come home tired from a job he hated and either watch TV and drink beer or go out with the boys. He made sure his family was taking care off, and his job was done. That was his whole purpose in life. He probably didn't say I love you much or hang around with you much, but you had a roof over your head, and you never missed a meal.

I prefer a responsible, tuff, hard worker dad over a loving lazy dad any time. Love doesn't bring food to the table. Love does not build a roof over your head. Love is not going to pay for your college tuition, and most important love is not going to help you get better from an illness.

My dad didn't help my mom financially at all. He was never around, so I never asked him for anything. At a low point in my life here in the USA, I decided to reach out to my dad for help, and he denied it. I have never asked for his help, but I was in a bad stage in my life, so I asked for help, and he didn't help me. I was disappointed, but I wasn't surprised. I wrote him a letter when I got sober and wished him well and told him he would never hear from me ever again. I told him how I felt and how he should learn to love more. I wished him well and told him that I forgave him, and explained to him that I understood that we all struggle in life and no one really knows what people go through life, and we all have life issues. I wished him well, told him not to contact me ever and wished he discovered peace and love within himself.

We have to discover the balance between love and responsibility. We have to know when love interferes with our responsibilities and vice versa. It's a very hard thing to discover and manage. I will struggle to find the balance my whole life. I need to provide for my family, but I also have to be a loving father. My dad wasn't any of those things, so I have to figure it out how to balance it myself. I overcompensate with my son. If I'm on my phone for more than five minutes, I think I'm a bad dad. I feel bad when I work late, and I'm not present to put him to bed. I always FaceTime him and say good night, but I still have a sense of failure. I should be there with him to put him to sleep. At the same time, if I don't work, I can't bring food to the table. Even writing this book I had a conflict within me. I only wrote it when I had free time at work or after he went to sleep. I deleted all social media and focused on him as much as I can. I don't have a full time job, so I'm always looking for better opportunities or side jobs to bring more money for my family. I have been working hard to become a better person and provide more for my family, but the opportunities of having a full time job haven't come out yet. Sometimes I feel like a failure for not bringing more income for my family, but I just keep grinding and working hard. My son is my number one responsibility in this world, and I need to provide a better future for him than the one I had. If it means that I'm not there to put him to sleep or I'm not there when they take his class photo then be it. I have to see the big picture and understand that I have to work as hard as I can to provide a better future for him. Right now that he is just a toddler is easier for me to keep looking for my dream job. He still little and he won't remember much. This gives me a great window of opportunity to look for a job that pays well, and I love. It might not happen, but all I can do is work hard and be a great human being. I have to work hard and be grateful for my opportunities. I believe that with my Girlfriend's help and with my talents I can achieve my goals before he turns five because once he turns five my window of opportunities will close. If I haven't achieved my dreams when he turns five, I would have to look for a job that will provide for my family. A job that I might not like but it will allow us to have a stable life. You may ask why five? Well at five years he would start kindergarten. This means he would not be part of my Girlfriend's preschool/daycare job anymore and we will have to adjust our schedules around his school. My Girlfriend job is far from where we currently live and far from Los Angeles where most of my job opportunities are. One of us would have to change jobs location or move from where we live to put him in a great school. So, for now, I have a couple of years to push myself and find that great job that would make us financially stable. This could mean that I may not be around much for my son, but it's for a better future.

If you are struggling with time and family, you have to see the pros and con of your time. If your baby is little, this is the best time to focus more on work and your financial future. Your kids won't remember their early years. This is your chance to spend long days at work and build more relationships to get more clients. You may miss his first steps, but you are working hard, so he has a car when he graduates and doesn't use his feet too much to travel. You may miss his first drawings, but you are working hard to have a manager position that would give you more vacation time and allow you to take your family on a trip to Rome and see the sixteenth chapel.

Those first five years are the most important years in terms of education and development. Sing, read and make activities during those years. But I'm sure he won't remember if you missed the first time he pooped his pants. So use those years to work as hard as you can to provide a better future for your family.

Always make time to read and play. It doesn't mean you have to read and play every day and all the time. It means that on Sunday nights you dedicate an hour of reading time before bed. Or Saturday morning go to the park. Also, your family has to understand that those Friday night meetings with clients would mean bigger bonuses for the family.

It's a hard task to balance love and responsibilities, but you have to try your best to do it. You have to be able to bring home the check to your wife, and read, and play with your son after dinner. It's a hard task but it's not impossible. It requires time, money and health. You have to be able to take care of yourself so that you can take care of your family. Use your health to make money. Use your money to make time. And use your time to make memories with your family.

**PS**. I kiss my son way too much. I'm sure I bug him a lot, but I don't give a fuck. I'm going to keep hugging him, kissing him and telling him I love him until I die.
I LOVE YOU SON!!!

Chapter 3

# THERE'S NO CRYING IN BASEBALL, ONLY IN FATHERHOOD

I can count with my own hands the times I cried before I became a dad. I cried when my grandma died when I was about 11 or 12 years old. Another time was when I was lighting up some fireworks, and I started running away from them then I hit I block and scraped my knee really bad. I wasn't crying because it hurt, I was crying because my mom didn't allow me to play with fireworks and I was worried she was going to get really mad. I also remember crying because I was lonely and missed my mom and family back in Guatemala. The worse was when I was on the bus heading home after a night of drinking, and I started to cry while drinking a six-pack of beer. I felt that my drinking was causing my depression and was ruining my life. I also cried when my Girlfriend almost left me because I was drinking too much. When I say crying, I mean really crying, tears, and tears are coming down my face for a long period of time. I'm sure I cried a couple more times as a kid when I got hurt, but that's pretty much it. I don't want to sound macho or anything, but crying wasn't my thing. I don't know if it was just my way of suppressing my emotions or I was just dead inside. Ha! Maybe my rough upbringings taught me to block my emotions and don't trust people, but it was rare that I cried. Now that I'm a dad, I cry like a little bitch! Last week I cried watching Shark Tank. That episode with the Latino guy who invents a lock that opens with your fingerprint. I think it's called Benji Lock. He started telling his story about being an immigrant, his struggles in life and that all he wanted was to provide for his family, and when he started crying, I lost it. I didn't start bawling, but I did shed some tears. No one was looking, so I shed some more. I don't know what it is now, but I get very emotional in different circumstances.

The first time I cried just like that was when I saw Toy Story with my son for the first time. I might be an adult with debt and no hair, but I'm just a grown ass kid. Till this day, my top two movies are Toy Story and The Sandlot. Toy Story changed my life; I was about 11 or 12 years old when Toy Story came out. Seeing it was a magical moment in my life. Toys that talk? What the fuck! Boom! My head exploded. I watched it over and over and over. I traveled everywhere with my Toy Story VHS. I went to see my uncle in Mexico, and I took my Toy Story

VHS and played it over and over. I believe the phrase "To Infinity and Beyond" has to be one of the best phrases of all time. Applies in so many inspirational ways. Whenever I feel down or stressed I put Toy Story or The Sandlot and they cheer me up or they just relax me. There have been many times when I put them on, and I fall asleep and nap during the movie. I don't nap, it's hard for me to nap during the day but somehow Toy Story and The sandlot do the trick. I guess I just feel happy and safe.

We don't watch too much TV, so I didn't put it on right away for my son to see, he must have been between 9-11 months when I decided to put it on for him. He needed to nap, I decided to put it on for him to watch and listen, so he and I could relax and then I could put him to sleep. "You got a friend in me" started playing and I started crying. I didn't cry for a long time, but I did have to wipe my tears off. My son didn't notice, and my Girlfriend wasn't present, so it was safe to cry. I never thought I would be sharing that moment with my son. My tears were happy tears, I was happy that he was there and I was there when he first saw Toy Story. Toy Story, the movie that changed my life and still one of my favorites of all time. My son and I sharing one of many precious moments a father wishes for. I shared and passed along one of my greatest joy in life. A happy memory passed down the bloodline. He might not like it as much as I like it but at least I shared that precious moment with him, and no one can take that away from us. Moments like those make you realize how great is to be a Dad. It doesn't matter that you didn't have a dad, it matters that he does. You will be there for those precious moments that remind you about your own childhood. Now you can pass down the joy of those happy moments in your life. Teach them to be happy and find joy in simple things. Show him different things that he might like. One day you'll be surprised to notice that he reacts just the way you do. Or he likes the same things you do. My son and I don't look much alike. He looks just like my Girlfriend. When he does something that only I do or likes things I like, it brings happiness and joy to my life. When he was a newborn, he started to raise his right eyebrow. Something I can do but my Girlfriend can't. That was my first proud moment as a dad. No other thing or person would bring more joy to your life than when your son makes you happy and proud. So, buckle up because it will be a sweet ride full of precious and proud moments that will bring a tear of cheer to your cheek. Or in my case, many, many tears.

**PS**. If the Dodgers win a World Series, I'm definitely crying.

Chapter 4

# PAPA SAYS, POW POW

My toddler son started to link people with what they say. For example, my brother is a huge Raider fan, so if you asked my son, "What does tio say?" he will answer, "Go Raiders." One time I was asking what people say, and when I asked him what does Papa say, he said, "Pow, Pow." At first I laughed, but later on, I started overthinking it and got sad and worried. I don't hit my son, but I do threaten to go pow pow on his hand if he touches certain things he's not supposed to.

Everything started when he was learning to crawl, he was near our TV set, and he brushed the Xbox and then Xbox turned on. He discovered how to turn it on. When you turn the Xbox on the Xbox logo lights up. He found that very interesting like any baby would, and he started to do it over and over again. We started to tell him to stop, and of course, he didn't stop. Then I started to tell him that if he continues, I will go Pow Pow on his hand and I slapped my own hand to show him what would happen if he continues. We continue this process until he figured it out not to turn it on anymore. Most of the time I'll raise my voice, and that would get his attention and even scare him. So when I asked him what Papa said, and his answer was Pow Pow, it didn't surprise me, but it made me think.

Am I doing the right thing and should my son fear me? I didn't have a dad or a male role model in the house to scare me or set me straight. I didn't know what I should be imposing on my son, so I just went with my gut. I asked my brother and friends if my son should fear me and the answer was always, absolutely! A son should have some fear from his dad, not that he is going to get beat up but fear of repercussion for their actions. Most of them said that their dads or moms had the "Look" or that "Tone of voice." When they heard it or saw the look, they knew they had messed up, and they knew they were in trouble. That fear has to be with you at all times, so you don't do stupid things or the wrong thing. That fear of disappointment, repercussion, losing your privileges or making your parents look bad in front of others. Every parent should have that look, or tone of voice to command some kind of order and discipline. I have it now. Not too long ago I used it without noticing. My son was about to hit my Girlfriend with his plastic bat when I said "Hey" loud, and he got a little scared, looked at me and stopped. During Christmas, I was putting up the tree lights, and he got behind me and was about to touch the power socket, and I said, "STOP" loud and clear and I told him if he touches that he would get an "AUCHI." So now Papa says "Auchi!" Babies and toddler are very smart individuals, so we always explain to him how some of his actions are not okay or even can cause him some harm. He knows not to touch the stove because it's hot and he knows not to turn the Xbox on. I prefer for him to be scare and safe than not scared and be touching electrical sockets.

Making your kids accountable for their actions is a big and important aspect of parenting. Even at the early stages they know and understand right from wrong. It's up to us to show them the path of a safe and righteous life. There will be mistakes on both sides along the way, but as long as we correct them and learn from them, you will be A-Okay.

Not having a dad around made me struggle with authority. I still do till this day. I don't like people telling me what to do, and I want people to do what I think it's right. Not having that male role model to set me straight allowed me to have this freedom and rebellion in my life. I used to disobey the rules at school, not wear the proper uniforms and even jump on the desk and run around. Good thing I was this cute fat kid when I was young, and most people couldn't get mad at me for long, but it was not ok for me to disobey the rules and give people headaches. Life is not fair. We need to understand that most of the time we need to adjust and adapt. Most of the time it's not going to go our way, and most people aren't going to do what we want them to do. We need to learn how to cope with that struggle and understand that we have to be a team player and not a one-man team. I want to teach my son that sometimes we need to be part of the solution, not the problem. We need to sacrifice our thoughts and opinions in order to have a good relationship with people and co-workers. We are not always right, and some of the times it's ok to do things their way, not our way.

I was a little fat troublemaker. The only time my mom was close enough to hit me (with a wooden spoon) was when I was about to do my first communion. I was too young, and my sense of responsibility was very low. She came home to take me to Catechism, and I was playing around with my neighbors on the roof of our house. That was my first strike because I was not allowed to be on the roof and when she pulled in the driveway she saw me on the roof of our house. Then she noticed that I was not ready to go to catechism and she also discovered I had lost all my books and my room was a mess too.

I'm sure she had a stressful day and had some anger built up from my sloppiness so when she saw me on the roof, saw my messy room, found out that I had lost all of my catechism books and I was not ready to leave, she had it. I have never seen her so mad. She went to the kitchen to get the spoon, and I ran to the back and climbed back on the roof and waited for her to cool down. She did calm down and told me I was not ready for that type of commitment, and I didn't do my first communion till I was 14 years old. I was the oldest and fattest kid when I did my first communion. She never really hit me.

I'm positive that events like that will happen with my son and I hope I don't have to climb roofs of houses or apartments looking for him. For now, I will keep explaining to him why he should not do things and how some of his actions can be hurtful for his being.

**PS**. If you ask my son what does papa say now, he would say "Go Dodgers."

Chapter 5

# I'M NOT ASKING YOU, I'M TELLING YOU

It's never the kid's fault; it's always the parent's fault. Every kid's actions are a representation of how their parents raise them. Even grown adults, we are a representation of how we were raised and our experiences in life.

I worked at a train that gave rides to kids for 5 years. I saw how kids and parents behave for 5 years. I saw every race, sex, religion, during winter, summer, and holidays. I saw how kids were treated and how the parents lecture them. From babies to teens, I saw it all.

My overall assessment is that you can't blame kids how they behave because it's not their fault. Their behavior is a product of how their parent raised them. It didn't matter the race, color, sex or religion of the kids; I always could tell when a kid was raised with discipline. Manners don't have a race, sex or financial status. Sometimes a kid can be hyper, but it's up to the parent to understand his own kid and have a plan for when they are in public.

It was sad to see how some kids didn't have their parent's full attention. Their parents would pay more attention to their cellphones than to their own kids. Those kids always did what they pleased. They would be pushing people around, touching and grabbing things that they weren't supposed to. Sometimes those parents would forget where their kids were and didn't even notice that they were gone. I'm sure you have seen those parents who are talking on their phone while their kids are hitting other kids or climbing places that they could get hurt. You become the responsible parent for those kids and have to grab the attention of their parent to do something about it. Many times parents would leave their kids in the train and forget about them. I would usually stay with them or tell them to stay in the carts and wait for the parent. They would usually come back but seemed like they had forgotten about them. Two instances I had to call security because the parents never came back. Most parents had well-behaved kids, but it was a big amount of kids that seemed like their parents didn't care or didn't want to be part of their behavior. It was more of a chore than a responsibility. Have you ever notice when parents are walking and looking at their phones or talking on the phone not paying attention of their kids and the kids are usually in the back following them minding their own business? There are a lot of those.

I love when a kid says please and thank you. It's not hard to say or teach. Teach your kids at a young age and keep reminding them to say please and thank you. It was a great moment when a toddler or a young kid said "can you open the door please" and when the ride was over they would say "thank you." Simple as that! Those two words aren't said enough these days. I try to remind my nephews and son every time we go out to say please and thank you. At Trader Joes, "Do you want stickers?" "Say, Stickers please." At Starbucks, "Did you say thank you after you got your drink?"

I also try for my son to say hi. It's the cutest thing when a toddler acknowledges your presence and says hi. It also teaches him that when we go places, we have to say hi. Whenever we go to my brother's house, I make sure he says hi and bye to everyone. One thing I hate with all my guts is when my son says hi to people without me telling him, and people don't acknowledge him. It makes me furious. How rude is that? If my son or other kids say hi to you while you wait in line for your fried rice you better say hi you Monster! A little cute toddler decided to acknowledge your presence and says hi to you, even waives his little hand and you ignore him and don't react or acknowledge him? Wow, you got issues. It happens more often than I would like to. So if a baby or a toddler says hi to you say hi back, please.

Your financial status, race and religion should never matter when it comes to manners. I try to say please and thank you as often as I can. When I talk to people, I try to refer to them as Sir and ma'am. If I don't know you personally, I would always call you sir and ma'am. Don't get me wrong; I talk trash to all my closest friends, but that is a level of trust that we have developed over the years. So let's set a good example for our kids when it comes to manners. It's not hard to say please and thank you. If the person doesn't react or doesn't have the manners to reply back don't be offended. His parents did not teach him well, and they don't have the level of common sense that you do. They are not polite, they don't have manners, but you do, and you are a better person for it. Trust me, if you do it's most likely your kids will to.

Another phrase that we started to say a lot is, "I'm not asking you, I'm telling you!" My son is going through the terrible 2s. I have seen it with my nephews and niece. My niece was the best. (she still is) Her thing at two years old was WHY? But, why? Why? It was hilarious, annoying and entertaining at the same time. This would be our conversation:

ME: I'm tired
NIECE: Why?
ME: Because I didn't sleep enough.
N: Why?
ME: Because I went to sleep late and you woke me up early to play with you.
N: Why?
ME: Because I'm unemployed and I'm turning in to your personal babysitter.
N: Why?
ME: Because you need a babysitter.
N: Why?
ME: Why you ask so many whys?
N: I'm two.

My son discovered "no," and he hasn't let go since. Everything is no. Every time we ask him to do things his reply is NO. One day I just told him, "I'm not asking you I'm telling you." I discovered that phrase, and I haven't let go since. My Girlfriend also uses it now. He has to understand that he has to pick up his toys after he is done and picking up his toys is not an option; it's a direct order. What we ask for him to do is not a request; it's a demand to be done at the moment. Most of the things we keep showing him to do are to set an example or a routine to help him develop and improve on his own skills. Picking up his toys and putting them away after he plays teaches him order and cleanliness. The house can be messy while we have fun and play but can't be messy at all times. Taking a shower at 8 pm gives him enough time for his hair to dry and for him to play a little more and have a healthy snack before 9 pm bedtime. He has to go to bed around 9 pm, so he is not tired when he wakes up early in the morning. So, when we say pick up your toys, and he says NO, I have to make sure he understands that what I'm saying is not a request that he can deny, It's direct order to be done immediately. The more you teach them and put a routine the easier will get for them to do things. My son doesn't fight us when he takes his bath or his nap. He understands that his bath, nap, snack time and clean up time is part of his routine and will happen whether he likes it or not. So he doesn't fight it, he goes along with it. I have to understand that I'm not his friend I'm his dad. Some instances he can do what he please but sometimes I'm not asking him, I'm telling him.

**PS**. Have him choose what he goes to sleep with. My son chooses his PJs and socks he is going to wear. It gives him a sense of independence.

## Chapter 6

# **105**

There's nothing worse than the hopeless feeling you get when your kid is sick, and there's nothing you can do to help him. That's how I felt in the emergency room when my son was a year old.

My Girlfriend is a teacher at a nonprofit preschool day care church. She has been working there for 10 plus years, and she is able to take my son with her every day, and he stays at the school while she works. It's a very nice place and very helpful for his education and learning habits. We are very lucky to have that luxury and everyone loves him so much. He is very lucky to have such wonderful teachers and friends that help him grow and learn at the same time. It's a great benefit for him and for us to have him there.

One of the bad things about having your son in a daycare or preschool is that they share everything, including germs.

Most doctors would tell you that fevers are a good thing. A fever is just your body fighting a virus. Most of us see fevers as a bad thing, and we want the fever to go down or go away ASAP, but that is not how your body works. A 101 or even 102 temperature is a good fever. How do I know that? Because we have been sent home many, many times by the doctor after we take my son in for a fever. They always say that a fever can last up to one week and that we just need to wait and let the body kill the virus. Even though I have a lot of experience with kids and my Girlfriend is basically trained to take care of kids we still get paranoid when it comes to our son. Parents should get paranoid when their son is sick or has a high fever; it's your kid! All you want is for him to be healthy and happy.

Every night I come home, and if my son is asleep, I stop by his crib make sure everything is ok and touch him. One time I touched him, and he felt hot. I went to take his temperature, and he had a 102 fever. We woke him up took all his clothes off and gave him some medicine to reduced his fever. It was a long Thursday night. When your child has a fever, it's recommended to check on him every two hours. For some reason, fevers tend to be high at night and low during the day, I guess fevers don't like you to sleep. My Girlfriend took him to the doctor that Friday morning and they were sent home to rest and get well. They just told her to monitor his fever and to go back Monday morning if it got worse. They came home, and he took a nap, and after an hour or two I checked him, and his hands and feet were a little blue-ish. I checked his temperature, and it hit 105. That ladies and gentleman would hit you like a rock in the face. It's a sinking feeling that you don't want to have. I immediately call the doctor until I got a response. They asked me if he was breathing fine and if he was having problems moving. I told them he was just a little blue and he had a 105 fever. He didn't have a problem breathing or moving. They immediately told us to go to the ER. We packed our stuff and went to the ER by our apartment. When we got there, there was another couple with their baby in front of us, and they were checking in too. We checked in and waited. That hospital was very nice, and it wasn't too busy, so we got in pretty fast. My guess is that they take priority for babies. Then they started to make some test, and that was the first time my son got his temperature taken by a rectal thermometer. It's a painful thing to see or do, but it's the most accurate way to do it. Hospitals usually use rectal thermometers. They did a couple more tests, and they also gave him medicine to reduce his fever, and we proceeded to a room where we waited for more tests and for his fever to come down. This whole process is very frustrating and traumatizing for a new parent. Every test they do, your kid suffers. Not necessarily physically but he doesn't understand that it's just for his own good. For him, it's just all these unknown people doing things to him that he doesn't want to do. He doesn't know that in order for him to feel better they have to run tests to help him get better. It's frustrating and sad to see your son cry and get scared every time they do a test, but you know it's for his own good, and you have to be tough for him and help the doctors and nurses in any way you can so they can figure out what's wrong with your child. We were there for about 8 hours, and we went home after his fever was stable. They really couldn't tell what was causing the high fever because all of their tests were coming out negative.

The doctor and nurses were amazing. They did a great job, and they treated us well. His fever was down and stable, and he looked better. We were heading home when we came across the other family with their kid, and we asked them what was wrong with their child. He had the same issue, 105 fever and they also couldn't tell what was wrong with him. All we can do was wait. We went home and monitored his fever. I went to buy a rectal thermometer to have a more accurate temperature reading. High fevers can cause brain damage and also can make you have seizures. We monitored him and kept an eye on him. He had a better night but still had a 101 – 103 fever. The morning after, my son had some kind of rash and when my Girlfriend saw him and saw the rash she immediately knew what he had. She took a quick look at him, and she said: "Ah, it's Roseola." Roseola is a contagious virus spread mostly within kids. Starts with a high fever for a couple of days and finishes with a rash. You won't know it's Roseola until the baby has the rash. The rash means the end of the virus. When the rash comes out, it means the virus is gone. And just like that, it was all good.

Those two days have to be one of the worst days of my life. That hopeless feeling you have is not a great one. You feel hopeless that you can't help your son at all, and all you can do is sit and wait. You have to let the doctors do their work and hope for the best. I can't imagine what other parents have to go through. My son only had a temporary virus. Some parents have worse situations than ours, and I can't imagine the pain they go thru. Seeing their kids sick and knowing they can't help. I don't wish this kind of suffering to anyone. I have nothing but admiration and a deep sense of respect for all those parents whose kids have a serious illness. They are brave and strong individuals.

Those two days I had to be strong. I had to show that everything was going to be ok. I had to trust the doctors and trust that my son would be ok. I had to show my son and Girlfriend that I was calm and that everything was going to be ok. They had to rely on me to be the strong male and give them support. I had to be strong and share my sense of calm to my son. Make him feel safe. Make him feel that his dad was there and it was going to be ok. Make him feel relax and calm. I had to be strong, relaxed, and calm for him. I had to be his Dad.

Moments of uncertainty can break you, but you have to be strong for your son. He looks up to you, and you have to show him that everything is going to be ok. Make him feel safe. A father has to make his son feel safe. Something that most of us didn't have growing up. So, hug your son tight and strong, give him a kiss and tell him everything is going to be ok because you are there to protect him.

**PS**. Shout out to all the doctors and nurses that help everyone in the ER. You guys do an amazing job. You are there to makes us feel better 24/7. Shout out to all the underpaid teachers and caregivers out there. I wish you guys would get paid what you guys deserve.

Chapter 7

# GROWING UP WITH AN IMMIGRANT PARENT

I feel bad for my son already. My Girlfriend was born and raised in Mexico and came to the USA when she was 16. I was born and raised in Guatemala and came to the USA when I was 16. My son has two immigrant parents. Not only am I an immigrant Dad but I also didn't have a dad around growing up, so I overcompensate being a dad. I want to be part of my son's life as much as I can. If I'm watching TV and he is around, I'll turn off the TV to play with him. I didn't have my dad around, so I want to be with my son 24/7. I'm going to be that parent that gets thrown off his son little league game and gets banned from the games. I always wanted my dad to be at my soccer games and my son is going to ask me NOT to show up to his. I'm going to try to be calm, but if my son is good and the ref makes a bad call, I'm going to express my feelings with my high pitch voice. Another thing that he is going to hate is when I compare him to me when I was his age. Man, poor him.

My mom was always working, and my grandma had health issues when I was young. My grandma basically was immobile because of her arthritis. So at a very young age, my mom made me very independent. My grandma helped raised me when I was a baby, but when I was around nine, I started to take care of her. I will help my mom shower her and other things. My mom had me do chores around the house to make me independent and be ready for my future. I always washed the dishes. She had a saying, "When I see you washing your woman's underwear at least I'll know you washed the dishes when you lived here." I don't remember much of my childhood, I remember very little before I was 11. I think something happened that made me block most of my memories. I do remember when I was about 9 or 10 years old I came to visit my brother here in the USA all by myself. My mom dropped me off at the airport in Guatemala, and my brother picked me up at LAX. I did very well on the way here to the USA and really bad when I went back. I remember that I flew back in American Airlines. They gave me so much free things with wings to make me stop crying, I cried like there was no tomorrow. That's how much I didn't want to go back to Guatemala. I was a sad little boy and to make it worse, the person next to me had a facial deformity. Nothing wrong with that but to a fat nine years old kid who is sad and crying isn't the best person to be sitting next too.

After my grandma died, it was just my mom and I. My mom was always working or partying so I did mostly everything by myself, this was my routine when I was 13 years old. I would wake up early to boil some water so I can put it in a bucket full of cold water to make it warm and use it to shower, I would get dress and then make me some breakfast. Sometimes my mom would leave me breakfast, but most of the time I would do some scrambled eggs with black beans. Then I would walk about four blocks to wait for the school bus, go to school and come home. If my mom didn't leave me money to buy dinner I would make some dinner, do my homework, and go outside and play with some friends. Then at night I would make me a snack and would get my uniform ready for the next day. My mom would come home around nine after a long day at work.

I'm not expecting my son to do all that but oh boy, he is going to get a lot of "When I was your age" from my Girlfriend and I. I'm sure you have a parent like that or know someone that has a parent that is like that. "When I was your age I would walk 200 miles to school, kill and cook my own dinner." I don't want to compare my situation as a child with his. I'm working hard to provide better resources, so he doesn't have to struggle the way I did, but there are things I learned along the way that I want him to learn too. I want him to be independent. Kids these days can't even make scrambled eggs or dress themselves. I had no choice but to become independent and grow up faster than my son will have to, but I want to teach him discipline and responsibilities. There is one bad thing that I developed by being too independent. I believe that I'm too independent. I have created a barrier that doesn't allow me to get hurt and can alienate me from others. "I don't need anyone in my life" That's my way of thinking. "I don't need any help from anyone. I can do it all by myself." It's good to be independent, but it's ok to have help from people in your life who love you. My childhood made me tough, but it also made me built a barrier that it's hard to climb. I'm still working on it. I trust people more, I let people in my life, and I let them see I'm vulnerable. I want to create a balance for my son between responsibility and accessibility. I want him to become my brother and me as one.

My brother and I were raised as a single child. He is 15 years older than me. He was raised old school by my grandma. He came to the USA when I was one, and I was raised new school as a single child by my mom. My grandma did everything for my brother; she cooked, clean, washed, iron his clothes, etc. My grandma even told my brother that the kitchen was no place for a man. The man had to work hard and provide for his family, and the woman took care of the kids, cooked and cleaned. My mom made me do it all. I cleaned, cooked, washed the dishes, etc. She made me understand that I can do it all and I didn't need a woman to clean, wash and cook. When I came to the USA, and I was living with my brother, I became his brother/wife. We lived in a two-bedroom apartment, and I did all the chores. He provided me with a place to live, and food and I cleaned, cooked, and washed our clothes. It was a fair trade. We complemented each other the way we were raised.

My Girlfriend and I grew up poor. We didn't have much growing up, and we want to pass that along to my son. We don't want to shame him for having better things that we did, but I want him to know the struggle we had in order to have better things. All I want in life is to provide better opportunities for my son and share with him how our lives were when we were kids. I want him to know that we can always survive with beans. I used to have beans three times a day. Freshly cooked beans from the pot for breakfast, bean soup with white rice for lunch and refried beans for dinner with bread. Growing up poor gives you a certain calm. You already know how to survive being poor. You are prepared if something goes wrong financially and you have to go back being poor. You know the struggles and how to maximize what you have. I want him to understand that and to know that sometimes we have to make sacrifices for the best. Only because we can afford something doesn't mean we should have it. We can live happy with the necessary.

My Girlfriend was raised very old school too. Her mom is one of the toughest individuals I know. I respect her very much. She worked in the fields picking up lettuce for years, she has never asked the government for help, and she has a lot of pride. She doesn't ask for help much just like me. When my Girlfriend and I started living together I had to explain to her that I didn't need a maid, I needed a Girlfriend. She wanted to do everything for me, and I didn't want her to do anything for me. She had to have dinner ready at night and laundry done by Saturday and so on. She was raised very old school. I told her I was raised very independently and she had to stop doing everything for me. I like to do things my way, and she was getting in the way. It also seemed like she had to do those things otherwise I would leave her. That's how she was raised. If you have old school parents or Latinos parents, you know how it goes. The dad won't eat until the mom serves him food. It's like he can't do it himself. She wanted to do that until I had a conversation with her. I need her for her company and love not as a maid.

I want my son to be independent. If he is hungry and we are asleep, I want him to make himself some breakfast, to know how to change a tire, to wash his own clothes and know where everything is at home. I want him to take action and not to wait for someone else to do it. I don't want him to boil water to put it in a bucket so he can shower. I want him to boil water to make oatmeal for breakfast without any help from us and I want him to wake up early and have everything ready for school. I don't want him to be alone all day long, but I want him to know how to cook just in case we aren't home. I want him to know that I'm always going to be there for him, but just in case I'm not, for him to be ok. I want him to be responsible for his well being.

As long as my son is not making any mental or physically harm to anyone he can be anything he wants to be. He can be an actor, writer, lawyer, janitor or a teacher. As long as that is his choice and he is happy with it, I will support him one hundred percent. At the moment I don't have a full time job and don't have health insurance or vacation time. The older I get, the more I know how important those perks are. It's sad to know that if I don't work my family doesn't eat. I just did my taxes and found out I had five jobs last year. I have to hustle to provide for my family. I'm still hustling to achieve my dream job, but the older my son gets, the more I need to have a more stable job. I need to have paid vacations to enjoy my family. I need health insurance for health emergencies and so on. When I worked in promotions, people would say they wanted to have my job. I would ask them what they did for a living, and they would respond, "My job is boring, I make plane parts." Then I would ask if they had health insurance and paid time off and they would say yes. That would be the main difference between my "cool" job and their "boring" job. Health insurance, paid time off, pensions, maternity leave, those are perks that most people take for granted. If my son decides to become a teacher, with days off and a pension I would be happy for him and his future. It's not about the glamour of what you do is what you do to provide for your loved ones.

I don't want to pressure my son with my stories when I was a child; I want to share the stories for him to know that by being independent you can achieve more in life. Someone who needs help and attention for basic life chores would have less time to concentrate on their abilities that can help their future. I want my son to understand that. If his dad was able to cook breakfast when he was nine, then he can make a buffet when he is nine. If his dad graduated high school with high honors, he can too. The world is his to conquer, and he should know he can do anything he puts his mind on. That feeling of accomplishment you have after you complete a task is an amazing feeling. This book would be one of those challenges for me. I'm writing this book so you can help yourself be better and more independent. I want you to accomplish your task and dreams. I also want my son to understand that if I can write a book, then he too can write a book and so do you.

**PS**. Till this day I can cook better rice than my mom and Girlfriend combine.


It took me eleven years to become a resident and 17 years to become a citizen. It was not an easy task, but I did it the right way, and I'm proud to be an American Citizen. There were moments when I didn't think I would ever become a resident or a citizen and I would get depressed. I was always afraid of white vans, and I didn't think I would ever get the chance to achieve my dreams. My brother was the first one to become a citizen, then my mom, and lastly, me. Becoming a citizen has to be one of the proudest moment of my life. I cried during the ceremony, and I'm grateful to this country for letting me be here and accomplish my dreams. I saw an interview with this Olympian who said she was representing two countries. Her dad was born in another country, and she was born in the USA. She said she was happy that she didn't have to choose a flag and was able to represent two countries. I got mad because, in my opinion, she should represent the country she was born in. Especially in the Olympics. The USA was sponsoring her, and she should be representing the USA all the way. Maybe she was being nice and didn't mean it the way I saw it, but I believe that we all have to be grateful for the country we live in. If you were lucky to be born in the USA, you are and will always be an American. My son is an American. He is not a Mexican American or a Guatemalan American. He is an American, and I hope he cheers for the USA every time they compete in anything. I love the USA, and I'm grateful to be living in a country where I can become anything I want. This is truly the land of the free and where dreams come true.

Chapter 8

# A, NOT PLUS

Why can't I call people fat, but everyone can call me shorty? It's a very bias situation going on here. I recently had a similar situation at my son's school. At his school, they do this nice parade for Halloween. It's a great little event that they do where all the kids do a parade and march around the classrooms and showcase their costumes. I like to attend and participate in this fun event. My son and I were dressed up as Charlie Brown and Linus. I was Charlie Brown since I'm bald and he was Linus. My son doesn't like to put anything on his head at all, so it was much easier to make him Linus. We were going through the classrooms showcasing everyone costumes when a teacher said "Hi chaparrito" to my son, then she said "Bye Chaparrito." Chaparrito is shorty in Spanish. I didn't get mad, but I wanted to turn around and say "Bye Gordita," but I didn't. I didn't do it because if I have had done it, I would have been the "Bad guy," the disrespectful parent that judges people. If you think about it, that teacher was judging my son by his height. He is short for his age, and he is the shortest in his class. It is understandable why she would call him that but it's not fair that she can judge my son for his physical attributes but I can't judge her for hers. I expressed my thoughts to my Girlfriend and asked if I can start calling that teacher fatty. She obviously said, absolutely NOT! Then I asked her to tell that teacher to stop calling my son shorty. If I can't judge her by her appearance then neither can she judge my son by his. It should be a fair trade, if you are describing my physical appearance, then I should be able to do it to you too. She talked to the teacher, and she stopped. I guess it's a cultural thing. Calling someone shorty is cute but fatty it's rude. She is not a bad teacher; she is actually very nice and caring teacher. In the Latino community, it is very common to call someone shorty. I'm sure she did it because she felt my son was part of her family, but it should be fair game or no game at all.

He is too young to have someone already telling him he is short. There is going to be plenty of people telling him that for the rest of his life. His uncles are tall so who knows maybe he turns out to be the tall one of the family, I doubt it, but it can happen. It's ok, I have plenty of experience dealing with height issues so I'll be there to guide him thru the short cuts.

What does A plus mean when they give grades? Or B plus plus? I don't get the plus. Why the plus? Just let

A be a good grade and D a bad grade. Or make them numbers. It should be 0 to 100 and done. No one can go above 100. I don't understand why you have to give a plus to someone who already worked hard for an A. Why do you have to tell an A student that another A student is better than them. Either you are an A student or a B student, stop it with the plus.

We can't compare kids with other kids. I used to hate it when my mom used to compare me with my brother. She would make me feel that I was stupid and my brother was smart. My brother had good grades, was an honor student growing up and I wasn't. I was the kid who didn't obey the rules and push the limits. My mom would always tell me how smart my brother was and how he always got A's and I didn't. Ugh, I hated it. Now that I'm older and I spent a lot of time with my brother and I got to know him more I see how we both are very different and it doesn't mean he was smarter or better than me he just liked school and I didn't. Simple as that! I wished my mom would have seen that and didn't cause me so much pain growing up always comparing me to my smart brother. He wasn't smarter than me he just liked to study and loved going to school, and I didn't. We are all different.

The same goes for our children. We can't compare them with siblings because every kid is different. Only because a kid has bad grades doesn't mean he is not smart. One of the biggest stereotypes that we have here in the USA is that Asian kids are smarter than everyone else. Not true at all. They do have better grades than most, but that doesn't mean they are all smarter than everyone else. Asians families are more dedicated than most, and they give a lot of priority to school and learning. Just like my brother and I, he liked to study, learn and go to school and I didn't like school or to study at all. Of course, he is going to have better grades than me. It's simple. If you dedicate time to study hard and learn you will have good grades and do better in school. I wish all of us will be as dedicated as most Asians families are to learning and studying but we are not the same. Some of us aren't wired like that.

I see the same thing is happening in my family. My nephew is very smart and good at school, and my niece doesn't like school, and her grades are not as good as her brothers. My nephew is very patient and likes to write and play video games. My niece is an artist; I believe she has raw talent. She is very good with people and very expressive and great with entertainment. It looks like my nephew will be the Lawyer in the family, and my Niece will be the Artist or Journalist of the family. They both have great potential in different aspects of their life. That's what we all need to find in our kids. We have to see their potential and push them to success. My nephew can be a lawyer, but he can also be a great writer. My niece can be a great journalist or a great painter. We all have different talents. It's our job as parents to discover those talents and encourage our kids to pursue them and reach their full potential. At the moment my son is very good with school, and he has a large knowledge of words, number, and expressions. He even knows sign language. They teach him sign language at school, he comes home, and he teaches me how to say the colors in sign language. Sometimes I feel he is just fucking with me but who knows; maybe he is telling me the truth. He is ahead of his class in terms of education but he lacks social skills, and he needs to be more independent. My son is book smart but not streets smart. We need to be both. We are happy with the progress that he does at school, but we are trying for him to improve in certain aspects of his life. He is way too young to guess what he is going to be in life. Couple months ago my Girlfriend said to me, "He loves animals. He is going to be a Veterinarian." Then I said, "He loves spoons too, he is going to be a waiter."

I will try not to compare my son to anyone. I want to help him find what he likes and what he is good at and achieve his full potential. I believe that in some cases kids are born to be something. Watching the Olympics and listening to those athletes say how they wanted to be an Olympic skater since they were little and their parents gave up everything so they can achieve their dreams is what I want to do. If my son comes up to me one day and says, he wants to be a baseball player I will do everything in my power to make his dream come true. Maybe along the way, he realizes he doesn't want to be a baseball player, but if he is willing to try and work hard at it, I'm in one hundred percent. Let's make his dreams come true.

When it comes to religion, I'm not religious at all. My opinions about religion may offend people, but I don't mind people's religious beliefs. I was raised Catholic, but I don't consider myself religious at all. My son was baptized because my Girlfriend wanted it, and I had no problem baptizing him or being part of the celebration. If my Girlfriend wants to introduce religion to my son, I'm ok with it. I want him to have options. I want him to have some sense of religion, and if he decides to follow it, I will support his decision. One thing I won't do is push religion on him. When he gets older, and he wants to stop going to church, or he decides not to have a religion I will be ok with that. I want him to make his own decision based on his experiences. I don't think because he doesn't go to church he will become a bad person. If we don't teach him good from bad he might, but for the moment, I don't mind if my Girlfriend shares her religious beliefs with him. He needs to experience them and make his own assessments along the way.

I want to let my son discovered what he likes and what he is good at. I can't push him to do something he doesn't want to do. I don't want to push my own agenda in to his life. I want to provide him with resources, not obstacles. I also want him to discover that achieving a goal is one of the hardest things to do. There is always someone better or faster than you, so you better be prepared and ready. The way we live now we give to many awards for everything we do. I wish we could be a little tougher and don't give awards for participation. We have to teach our kids that sometimes we win and sometimes we lose. When we lose, we have to work harder to win. Sometimes we get a D so we have to study harder to get an A. We can't all be A student. Some of us are B, and that's ok. C and D student can be bad at school, but they can be great in the stock market and make millions of dollars more than the A student will. When I took my SAT test in High School, I scored average. What no one realized was that the test was an average of two scores. One score was for math, and the other was for grammar or English. I scored 800 in math and 400 hundred in grammar. English is my second language, and I'm still learning it (thank you spellcheck). So when they average the score, they saw that I was average. I was average overall, but I was on top in math.

Pay attention to what your kids do and like. You may have the next Steven Spielberg or the next Barack Obama. Who knows, maybe you have the next Nobel Prize winner In Science. Who knows?

**PS**. One thing I knew for sure I was never going to be. An NBA player.

## Chapter 9

# BOOZE & CHILDHOOD

For what I heard my dad was a go get him from the streets kind of alcoholic. He would disappear for days, and sometimes people would have to go get him from the bars and streets. My mom didn't mention if he would beat her up or that he was a bad person, but he was a full-on alcoholic. He quit drinking when I was a little boy, but he was not part of my life.

I believe my mom was a working alcoholic. She was a loving mom, but she would drink and party way too much. Sometimes her partying and drinking would affect me. A couple of time she left me by myself at the house, and she would go party the night away. As I got older, I realize that she tried to be a good mom, but she still was struggling with her alcohol demon. I think she quit drinking while I was here in the USA but I'm not really sure when she did. My mom tried her best to give me a great life, but she had personal, and financial problems. She provided food, housing, and pleasant memories. She is not a bad person at all, and she loved me very much, but her drinking was a problem in our lives. It's funny to see how she quit drinking and became very religious. She went from a drunk to a saint. I'm sure you have people like that in your family or know someone like that; I don't mind that at all, the way I see it is that religion saved her life. I prefer to have a religious annoying mom than a working alcoholic mom. I love my mom with all my heart, and I appreciate all the sacrifices she did for me. She never hit me, she provided food and shelter, and we took some vacations early on when she had money. I don't judge her anymore because believe me I'm not a saint either. I'm not even close to being a perfect person. Not at all my dear.

I'm not here to tell you to stop drinking. We are all different, our DNA is different, and we all have different issues to deal with. What alcohol does to me is different to what it does to you. I'm not here to tell you why you should stop drinking at all. I'm here to tell you why I stop drinking. My brother drinks, he has a house, takes a vacation and has an amazing family who loves him very much; he achieves his goals and has a great job. He is one of the most caring and loyal people you would ever meet, and alcohol doesn't affect his life at all. His dad was worse than mine, and my mom partied more when he was young, and he turned out to be an amazing human being. We are all different.

Me on the other hand, it's a totally different story. If you met me between 2011 and 2013, I apologize with all my heart. Those were my worse and last drinking years. I was an annoying, self-destructive prick drunk. It wasn't always like that; I had great drinking days and even great drinking memories. At one point my drinking brought me success. I met different people and had great relationships with many people, but as the years passed by, my drinking brought me depression and inner pain. I lost jobs and lost friends. I never did wrong but who wants to be friends with an annoying drunk? I wouldn't want too. My mom told me one time that drunks have a ghost who protects them. I believe I had one looking out for me. There were plenty of times where I didn't know how I got home. I was an immigrant for many years. I didn't have a license and didn't own a car. In a way, it was a blessing. A couple of times I had to take three buses to get home, and I still don't have any recollection how I got home. Around 2010 I knew I had a problem, I admitted it, and it took me two years to quit drinking. My first step was to stop blaming my parents for my failures and my drinking. I used to blame my dad and mom for my drinking. Finally, I realize that they never gave me a beer to drink, they never took me out to a bar, they never gave me money to buy alcohol, and they never encourage me to drink. My mom saw my pain and knew that I was an alcoholic way before anyone did. I'm guessing she had experienced the same and didn't want me to take the same path. I never listen to her because she wasn't the best person to tell me to stop drinking. Her way of thinking was and still is old school and her advice was very wrong and not useful for me. One time she literally told me that I should have a kid so I can stop drinking. That has to be one of the worse advice anyone has given me. WOW! I still don't know how she could think that way, but I'm guessing she just wanted me to stop drinking. I'm glad I laughed at her advice because at that moment I would have ruined that child's life if I had one. I was 28 at the time, and it would take me about three more years to stop drinking. I'm glad I had that ghost taking care of me, and I survived those last years. My last years of drinking I was obese, broke, no car, renting a room and no real future. I was a drunken mess. I had pain and sadness within me. I didn't love myself. I was destroying myself little by little.

It was a two-year struggle trying to quit. I understood that no one but me would help me. I stopped blaming my parents for my failures and drinking. Then I started to believe and love myself and one day I finally did it. I had it! I was tired of waking up with hangovers and never having money. I was an alcoholic, but I didn't drink every single day. No one ever had to go and get me from the streets. I paid rent and had an ok life but it wasn't going to take me anywhere, and I knew it. I would drink on holidays or days off, but I could drink all day and night. I didn't drink every day, but when I did, I really did. So one day after a couple of days of drinking I decided to stop, and I did. I knew that if I didn't stop I would end up on the streets. I wanted to be a better person, I wanted to have better things, and I wanted to be a better example for my family, so I quit. I quit drinking on April 15th. April 15th is an important day for many reasons in my life, so I decided to quit that day, and I haven't looked back. I quit cold turkey. It was not easy, but I achieved my goal to quit. I took it day by day, and I went to a couple of AA meetings but discovered that those meetings were not right for me. Those meetings showed me how some people had it worse than I did and I was blessed to quit drinking when I did, but those meetings lowered my self-esteem. A major thing that helps me realized I made the right choice was the money. In six months after I quit drinking I had a better job, a car and an apartment. If that is not a sign I made the right choice, then I don't know what is. I'm glad I quit because the next year my Girlfriend got pregnant.

Things happen for a reason. I met my Girlfriend at the end of my drinking days and bless her heart she stayed with me. She struggled right along myself with my drinking, and for that and other reasons, I love her with all my heart. I stayed sober and continued to strive for better. I want to be better and provide more for my family because my Girlfriend and my son deserve it. We all do.

My parents drinking made a huge impact in my life. I became an alcoholic by choice, not because my parents were alcoholics. No one made me an alcoholic, I chose it, and I struggle in life, but now I know right from wrong. Those drinking years showed me the dark side. Now I thrive on the good side for a better future for my family and me.

I believe alcoholism is a destructive disease. I don't wish that on anyone. I was in a rabbit hole that was hard to come out off. My drinking brought me a lot of pain and self-destruction. It also brought a lot of pain to my loved ones. I'm lucky that I stopped and turned my life around. I was destroying my life little by little. I lost jobs, friends and I got in to a lot of credit card debt. I still owe money on my credit cards due to my drinking, and it's a price I have to pay. My credit card debt is a reminder of my dark days and every day it passes by I'm happy I quit drinking, and I turned my life around. I'm a better person and a better role model for my loved ones. If you are struggling in life, know that there is hope and you too can turn your life around. Do it for yourself. You deserve better.

Would I let my son drink or do drugs? I can't stop it, but I can prevent it. I'm going to share my experiences with him; I'm going to be honest, and blunt about my alcoholism. I do believe alcoholism it's a gene that we carry around. I would share with my son every time I can that his dad, grandma, and grandpa were alcoholics. I would tell him about the great times I had with friends. How fun was to watch concerts and baseball games while buzz and I would share with him how lonely I felt when I was drinking by myself at night. I would share that drinking made me feel confident at the beginning and depressed at the end. I can only share my experiences with him for him to know. I will try to scare him with my black out stories, but that's all I can do. I would also advise him that if he decides to drink or do drugs that he should do it with people and friends he trusts. I was blessed to have great people around me while I drank. I could have been robbed, raped or killed. I want him to understand that if he decides to drink or do drugs he better have good friends that can take care of him if something happens. It's like sex, if you are going to have sex wear a condom. I hope he sees the mistakes I did, and he doesn't duplicate them. I hope he understands that he has a higher risk of becoming an addict than most people do. It's my job to share and make him understand that his actions will have consequences. He will make mistakes, but it's my job for him to be safe and sound. I will make sure he sees and understands the dangers of alcohol and drugs. I can't be there 24/7 with him, but I can get in to his mind and paint a picture of what can happen. I hope he doesn't drink or do drugs but if he does I hope he does it responsibly and with great friends.

As for me, I don't want to go back to my drinking days ever. I don't miss it at all. I drink non-alcoholic beer if I'm at a family party or if I'm watching a game. Most places now carry non-alcoholic beer, and most beer companies have a non-alcoholic beer. Trader Joes has a couple of great cheap non-alcoholic beers if you ever want to try them. One six-pack would cost me around 7 dollars and can last me one to two weeks. I don't miss my drinking days at all, and I'm a better person for it. I have to set a good example for my son and my nephews. They look up to me, and I have to set the bar high for them.

**PS**. The best drinking bars are Irish pubs. There is always someone drunker than you. So hit up an Irish bar once in a while. There's a great Irish pub downtown LA called Casey's Irish Pub. They make their own pickle juice. Watch out for the stairs.

Chapter 10

# YOU HAD A MALE ROLE MODEL

You may have not had a father around, but maybe you had someone who was your male role model. It could have been, your older brother, uncle, cousin, a TV dad, or your own mother. Your male role model was someone you look up to or someone who took care of you.

In most cases, it was always that older brother. That's whom my male role model was and still is to date. One day I want to be as good as a person and dad that he is. For most of my childhood, I didn't know that my brother was taking care of me from the USA. My brother moved to the USA when I was one year old. We used to visit him almost every year and when the visit was over, I didn't want to go back to Guatemala. I always wanted to stay with my brother. He would send my mom money to help us out and to support me. For what I heard the money was never well manage, but I made it out in one piece. My biological dad never helped my mother financially, but my brother did. Without me knowing my brother was already my male role model.

My uncle was another male role model for me. He was basically the weekend dad. He knew my mom was struggling so he would have me at his house a lot he even took me on vacations with them. He has two kids, and my cousins were like my brother and sister. We would spend vacations and every other weekend together. We spent most of our childhood together. My uncle's wife was of German descent. Her parents were German. So, my cousin, Otto looks very German like. Otto is tall, skinny with blonde hair and light eyes. His sister Cristina looks like me, dark skin with amazing curly hair. When we used to vacation together, they always thought Otto was the cousin, and she and I were brothers. My uncle would take me everywhere with them. He was a very old school man, so he didn't say much or express his feelings, but he was a true man. He worked hard and provided plenty for his family. They had a big amazing house, and he had a great job. I would love to stay with them because I could eat all the stuff my mom could never afford. I ate so much salami when I stayed with my uncle that I think he is responsible for me being so fat. He also introduced sports to us. He was a huge soccer fan. He is one of the reasons I follow Barcelona's soccer team so close till this day. My uncle was my part-time dad, and I would always love him for that. He passed away a couple of years ago, and I couldn't make it to his funeral because I had just become a Citizen and didn't have a passport and by the time I would have gotten it he would have been buried. So I couldn't attend his funeral, but I wrote him this letter for my cousin to read it out loud before they buried him:

```
"Hello everyone, this is Jose, Violeta's
youngest son, the short one. I couldn't
get my passport on time, so I'm writing
this words for my Uncle Ruben.

For what my brother has told me my Uncle
was the father HE never had. He taught
him how to be responsible, how to be a
good worker, about sex, sports, and how
to be a good family man.

For me, my Uncle was a father figure,
not as much as my brother but he was
there for me. Thanks to him I got to
travel all over Guatemala. Every time I
listen to "Burbujas De Amor" sang by
Juan Luis Guerra I always remember going
to the beach with my uncle and cousins.
They would play his songs over and over.
I love Juan Luis Guerra now, but back
then I used to hate his songs. A lot of
my childhood I spent it at my uncle's
house. Every time I would spend the
weekend at his house Otto, and I would
```

eat all the salami he had. He must be the reason I was so fat. One time we got in trouble because he just had bought some and we ate it all, and we didn't leave anything for anyone. Thanks to him I got to spend time with Otto and Cristina, and I got to see how different they are from each other and how talented they are in their own way. My uncle and his wife saw their unique talents and help them used them to be what they are now. Otto is an artist, singer, musician, and talented pianist. Cristina is very smart and creative. I still remember all the art she used to do with chocolate. She is a great cook and lawyer now. Dang chocolate and salami, no wonder I was so fat.

My uncle opened the doors of his house to me and let me be part of his family. He gave me a brother in Otto, a sister in Cristina and a Dad in him. I would never forget all the great memories we had together, and for that, I thank my uncle and his wife. Thanks for letting me part of their family.

With death comes a lot of pain. It also allows us to reflect on life. In the life we got and how we have to be better human beings. I believe that we have to help ourselves before we can help others. We have to be better fathers, sons, and husbands. We have to find the balance in life. It's not easy I'm still trying to figure it out myself. We are not perfect, we are humans, and we all make mistakes. My uncle made mistakes but he was a better man and father than mine was and for that, I give him thanks. One day I want to be like my uncle, maybe better. Now that I'm a father all I want is for my son to be better than me in all aspects of life.

Thanks for taking the time and listen to these kind words.

Jose and his 440."

    Not having a dad around makes a huge impact in a kid's life. I have struggled with panic attacks, anxiety and insecurities all my life. I'm always scared for some reason. I'm not a confident person even though I may look like one. I guess, I always thought I was not good enough. I never had a strong, confident role model that I could look up too. I had to learn how to talk to girls by myself. I had to figure out about sex, alcohol and how credit and credit cards work by myself. The impact of my dad being absent has been huge in my life. It took me a long time to figure out that I struggle with anxiety and self-confidence. I have been able to work with my issues, and I'm better now, but I still struggle with my daddy issues. I'm barely trying to accomplish my dreams and only because my son was born. When my son was born, it gave me another reason to succeed in life. His birth gave me a confidence and a drive I have never had. My love for him has made me be a more driven guy to provide better things in life for him. At the end of the day, all I want is to be his role Model. I will make mistakes along the way, but I will be there to provide confidence and support for him. I will teach him about sex, sports, alcohol, credit cards, fitness and maybe some writing and acting skills. My number one job and responsibility in life is to be a dad, and I'm up for the challenge.

My brother is my friend and my dad at the same time. He has been my role model since I was little. He continues to be my role model since I got to the USA. He is not perfect but who is it? He is strong when he needs to be and compassionate when he needs to be. He takes care of his family and provides a better future for his kids. People love to hang around him and be his friend. He loves to have parties and makes everyone welcome at his house.

He is old school, he was raised like that, and he still goes about his business that way. We disagree a lot in the way we think but I always ask him for advice, and he is my number one go-to guy. He makes me mad a lot, but now I know the reason why I get so mad at him so much. I get very mad because his opinion and approval means the world to me. I care so deeply for him that when he doesn't agree or understands me, I get frustrated and mad, just like anyone would get mad at his or her own dad. In the end, all I want to do is make him proud.

My brother is the American Dream. He came to the USA by choice to learn English. At the time my mom was not struggling, and he didn't need to come to the USA, but he did. He came to learn English and study his passion, which is computers. He came to this great country of ours, learned the language, study hard, worked hard and never asked the government for help. He worked for an insurance company from the bottom up. He started in the mailroom and worked his way up to the IT department. Then his department got outsourced, and he stayed to train the new people taking his job. He started working for the school department doing overnights, and now he is a supervisor in his company. He owns a house, and his family adores him. If that is not the American Dream, then I don't know what is.

If it weren't for my brother, I wouldn't be here writing this. His guidance and support have helped me my whole life. I don't know where I would be without him. I love him for that. I'm very lucky that he lets me be part of his life. I know he always has my back.

My brother has taught me how to be a Dad without my Dad.

**PS**. Shout out to all those role models out there. To the big brothers and sisters. To the uncles and cousin who were there when our fathers were not. To the teachers that care about our futures. Lastly, to all single mothers who had to become a mom and a dad.

## Chapter 11

# LIFE IS SHORT, JUST LIKE ME

Now that I'm a parent I have learned to relax. I had too. I still have trouble enjoying the moment. Enjoying the present. I'm always looking in to the future. Always planning what is coming up next and not concentrating in to what is happening at the moment. I don't know if it's my anxiety or what but I need to know my next step, I need to know my schedule ahead of time and plan for it. I don't like when people can't make up their minds and leave everything until the last minute. I make mental schedules even for simple things like going out for lunch on Saturday or heading out to see the family. I hate being late even if it is for family events. If I say I will be there at 10 am for the party you know damn right I will be there at 10 am. So the night before I start making mental notes to be on time. I start planning at what time we will have breakfast, what time my Girlfriend should get ready and what time we should leave to be there on time. I'm one of those who can get ready super quick. I take a shower, eat, and get dress all in 20 minutes. I don't take long showers, and I always eat super fast no matter the going to steal my food. I was raised like that. My mom used to say to me, "You have 5 minutes to eat, or I will leave you" so I got used to eating fast. If we go to a restaurant, I'm usually the first one to finish my meal. Now that I'm a parent eating fast is an advantage. When your kids are babies or toddlers, you don't have much time to enjoy a meal, especially at a restaurant. If you are at eating at a restaurant, you can't enjoy a meal as you used too. You may have 30-40 minutes max to eat. This includes the whole time at a restaurant. Your baby won't stay still for long. So you get used to eating fast. What we do now is that my Girlfriend feeds my son while I eat and once I'm done eating, she would eat while I feed my son. It's all about teamwork.

I like structure, and I don't like breaking it. My son usually takes 3 hours naps. So we plan around it. He needs his naps especially now that he is a toddler and he is developing his body. His schedule is usually the same during the weekdays. He naps between 12 pm and 3 pm. We try to stick to the same routine during the weekends too. When you become a parent, you will notice that your kids will wake up early no matter what day it is. It usually stays like that until they grow older. My son usually wakes up between 6 or 7 am no matter what day it is. So we like to keep his schedule the same, so he is not tired. I'm always planning around his naptime. I usually leave a nap window between 12-4pm. If we need to go somewhere or attend an event, we plan it around his nap schedule. We don't do anything between 12-4pm and try to be home for him to rest. You as parents will enjoy naptime as well. It's our free time. We usually watch TV, exercise, and pay bills or we also nap with him to rest too. If you don't have a nap schedule you should create one it will benefit your kids and you as a parent.

Another aspect I have learned to improve is when I drive. I used to get mad all the time while driving but I have learned to control that too. Los Angeles has one of the worst traffic in the USA and a lot of careless drivers. One thing I hate with all my guts are drivers who don't use their blinkers. It's worse when they cut you off, and they don't even have the decency to use their blinkers. It used to make me furious. If someone would cut me off without putting their blinker, I would move to the side speed up and try to see their dumb faces. I used to get road rage. It's a bad thing, but if you live in LA, you have done it at some point in your LA commute life. Once I became a dad, I learned to let all that go. I decided that I was putting myself in danger when I had road rage. You never know who might be driving and what they might do to you. I didn't want to put myself in a situation where I could harm myself. My son needs me in his life. I can't have road rage take control of my actions and put my life in danger. It took me a while, but I'm better now. I used to get mad and crazy, but now I just let it go. I prefer to let it go and come home safe to be with my son. Everything I do will affect my son's life, so I prefer to be safe than sorry.

When I was younger I had that free I don't give a fuck mentality. Somewhere along my adulthood, I forgot it. Now that I'm a father I have learned to let things go. I used to get mad for many stupid reasons. I try not to overthink things now, and I try for situations not to affect my moods. I try not to worry about things I can't control or things that I can't change. If I made a mistake, I don't let it bother me like it used to. If I have a job interview or an audition, I don't let it bother me. I still get nervous if I have an audition or a job interview, but I don't let it haunt me anymore. Sometimes I would overthink it the night before, and I would not be able to sleep well. My past used to hunt me as well; I used to overthink my past and would affect my present. I don't let that bother me now. I can't change the past but I'm a better man now, and I just want to work hard to be a better father for my son.

Another thing I have learned to let go is people's actions. They used to bother me, or they used to affect my way of life. I would worry if people got mad, when people did wrong with their actions or if people would be mean. I grew a pair, and I don't let it bother me anymore. Confrontation is sometimes a good thing, but I used to avoid them. I would bottle up my feelings and not speak up if something bothers me or affected my way of living. One recent incident that used to bother me a lot was our parking situation at our apartments. Our apartment building is on a major street, and there is limited parking. The side streets are residential, and you need a parking permit to park on them, and we only get one designated parking space in our building. I usually work at night, so my Girlfriend would have to park on the street when she got home otherwise I would not find parking when I got home late at night and would have to park on the side street and get a parking ticket. There are two guys who live together in our apartment building that park awful. They own two little cars, and they park them like they were eighteen-wheelers. It used to bother me a lot because my Girlfriend would have to park up the street and had to walk down to our apartments because this two fuckers will park like idiots. Another thing they like to do is not use their own designated parking space in the building and park on the street. So not only they park like idiots, but they don't use their own designated parking space in the building. That just means they are pricks and they park like that on purpose. Why wouldn't you use your own parking space in the building? A couple of times I left them notes for them to park better. I never did any harm to their cars just left them notes for them to park better. I think they might have figured it out because one day my car got egged. I never did anything to their car I just left them notes. They have gotten better because some other neighbors started to park outside and not let them park like they used to do. I have left notes one or two times more, but I have learned not to let it bother me anymore. It's not worth it. I can't change their actions. I don't care how they park anymore; I don't let it bother me anymore, one day Karma will get them back. If I let it bother, me they win. They park like that to mess with people and if I let them bother me they win. So I don't care. I just let it go now.

Not having that father figure never gave me that confidence to stand up for myself and confront people if they were doing wrong but I do now. This has helped me at my job. I don't let people dictate my work, and I don't let people's actions affect my work either. I stand up for myself and try to do a good job, so no one has a bad thing to say about me. I'm always asking my bosses on ways I can improve and how I can become a better worker. That helps me have a point of reference in case I'm doing a bad job. That way I can fix the problem if there's any. I stopped caring what people thought about me and concentrated on my own actions. It's not about what people do but what I do. It has helped me a lot in my professional life.

Everything we do, as parents will affect our kids. I have learned to let things go so I can focus on my son more. When I'm with him, he deserves my full attention and concentration. I can't be thinking about my job or if I got cut off in traffic and almost crashed. Life is too short to be worrying about things that happened in the past or things I can't control. Once I step into my house I have to leave all my personal and professional problems outside; I can't bring them home. My family deserves better. Life is short, let's enjoy it.

**PS.** Don't get offended if I ever flip you off on the freeway; it's not personal. I would flip my own mother off if she ever cuts me off and doesn't put her blinker on.

## Chapter 12

# TIPS & TRICKS.

At the moment a ticket to go to Disneyland here in California goes from $97 on a regular day to $134 on peak season. A kid 10 and up pays a regular ticket. So when my Girlfriend said we should take our ONE-year-old son to Disneyland, I started laughing.

Unfortunately, we live paycheck to paycheck, so I try to maximize our budget. My Girlfriend said that we should take our one-year-old son to Disneyland. That's an unnecessary expense. My son doesn't want to go to Disneyland, my Girlfriend does. My son was one, give him a plastic spoon and he is the happiest baby on earth. He doesn't know who Mickey is and he doesn't want to be standing in line for hours for a one-minute ride. Neither do I. So, for now, we are not going to Disneyland or Universal Studios until he specifically asks for it. Until my son says to me, "Father, I want to go see Mickey Mouse, Cars, and experience the New Star Wars ride in the happiest place on earth located in Anaheim California," then we will go.

If you are going to have a party for your kids first birthday, I hope you understand that the party if for you, not the baby. Your one-year-old baby is not going to remember the party, and he is not asking for a party or any gifts. We took a trip to Chicago for my son's first birthday. I got a Minions piggy bank and we put 20 dollars in it every month on the day of his birthday and we use that for his birthday. We also put extra change we have or tips I get here and there. We saved $500 for his first birthday, and we used that for the hotel in Chicago. We stayed there for a whole week, and we had a blast. It was also my Girlfriend first time on an airplane, so it made it more special. It was my sons and Girlfriend first time on an airplane. It's nice to have parties. Families get together, you get presents, food, etc. but they are also a hassle. We had a party for his second birthday, and it was full of headaches and the money we spent we could have used it to buy him a lot of clothes and other things he needed. It was not worth it. If you have the extra cash to have, a party go for it. Throw the party and enjoy it. But if you have a tight budget use the money you were going to use for the party and buy your son clothes, toys, and other things he might need.

Don't get a diaper BAG. Trust me! We were doing our baby shower wish list online, and my

Girlfriend selected a J Cole diaper bag she liked. I chose a diaper backpack. I suggested for her to get a diaper backpack too but she ignored my idea. I tried to explain to her that the diaper backpack would be helpful and the diaper bag would restrict one of her arms. She got her J Cole bag. Her diaper bag cost $70, and my diaper backpack was $40. Let's just say that at the end she ended using my backpack more than her diaper bag. A diaper bag needs to be carried on one had or across your shoulder, and it lays next to your waist. When you are carrying your newborn places inside the car seat you need both arms free; you need flexibility. A diaper bag doesn't give you much flexibility. If you have a diaper backpack, you have both arms free and more flexibility to carry the car seat or put the stroller in and out of your car. So, if you guys are considering an expensive diaper bag, get a backpack! Trust me; you will like it more in the long run.

Tell everyone not to get shoes for your newborn baby. Newborn shoes are the cutest useless things you can get anyone. They won't use them! I know they are cute but get something more useful, please. Tell your family to use the money they were going to spend in cute newborn shoes and give you a gift card for Costco or target. My son had like 5 pair of shoes when he was born, and he uses one pair maybe twice. They grow up so fast, and babies don't use shoes much. So, say no to baby shoes and say yes to diapers.

Another great gift that will be useful for years to come are shampoos and lotions. They usually are sold together and trust me you will always need them for years to come. More shampoos and fewer shoes.

Get a Costco card if you don't have one. Costco is great for many reasons including diapers and wipes. The diapers go on sale often, and you can stock up. My Girlfriend didn't have a card but she has one now, and she is an executive member now. There was an occasion that she thought the diapers were a little expensive at Costco and she saw a sale at target, and she bought a box of diapers for about five dollars less. It was the same brand name and same quantity. She opened them up and started using them and discovered that those diapers were of less quality than the ones at Costco. Costco products are better. Even if it's the same brand name, companies made special products for Costco. You can compare yourself. Buy a box of diapers at Costco and then buy the same ones somewhere else. You will see the differences. Become a Costco member. The benefits you get as a parent and as a member are infinite.

    If you have nephews or nieces or friends with little kids, start getting dibs. Start asking them to save you their kid's things. When my nephew was two, I bought him an original Dodger jersey and my son uses it now. My cousin is about to have a baby, and my son needs a new car seat, so I'm giving my cousin my son's old car seat. Things like car seats, jerseys, jackets, Halloween costumes, baby booster and high chairs are expensive, and you can use the ones your family doesn't use anymore. Most of them will be in great condition, and since most of them were used by family and friends, you know where they have been. There is no shame in using hand me downs.

    Get a dash camera. You are driving with the most important person in your life now, make sure you are protected and have evidence in case of an emergency. I got my dash cam for about 50 dollars, and I love it. We recently got rear-ended. Luckily it was not a big impact, and everything is ok. My dash cam captured the impact, and my insurance used it for proof of impact. So get a dash cam, you never know when you will need proof.

Always ask yourself, is this a necessity or a luxury? Only you know what's best for you and your family. The more you save, the better. You never know when you will need extra cash.

## Chapter 13

# HAPPY FATHER'S DAY, YOU GET A BREAK!

I have been around a lot of Dads during father's day. Most dads don't get what they really want on father's day. A friend of mine once told me that all he wanted for father's day was three meals and some quiet time.

That is a genius idea. This should be a rule or a trend. If you are a responsible and lovely parent, you are working hard, always with your kids, always doing something for your kids or doing chores with your kids. On father's day, you should get a day off. This applies to moms too. Moms are 24/7 with their kids or doing stuff for their kids. Moms would say, "All I want to do for mother's day is be with my kids." BULLPOOP! They are always with them, have a day off.

So from now on, this is what every parent should do for the other parent, or if the kids are grown do it for your parents. Feed them and let them have 24 hours of freedom. Rent a room for at least two days and send them room service. Simple as that! Every responsible parent wakes up early, makes meals, washes dishes, feeds the kids, dresses the kids, cleans the house, works, takes the kids to school, pick them up, soccer practice, diaper changes, nap times, snack time, story time, shower time, puke time, annoying songs time, teenager times, wash the clothes, and deal with the in-laws. All this, every single day! So on mother's day or father's day give them the gift of freedom. Rent a room and let them sleep late, watch anything they want to watch, give them cash to order in or room service. Let them curse and fart, be naked and loose. Let them be single and free for one day. Be able to wake up at any time, not to worry about anything, sleep and eat all day has to be the best gift any parent can have. You can be with your kids any other day.

So, on father's day, take a break!

**PS**. If you are on a budget, you can always rent a room the following weekend.

# FROM: Me
# TO: You

Thank you! I want to thank you from the bottom of my heart for reading this book. If this book helped you in any shape, or form I did my job. If some of my struggles in life helped you, I did my job. If you laughed or cried, I did my job. If you didn't like my book, I did my job too. If you think my writing was poor and now you know you can write a book well, I did my job. If this book gave you a point of reference on how to be a dad, my job is done.

I wanted to share with you my life experiences so you can see my struggles and maybe help with your own. I hope some of these stories were helpful. I'm not a doctor or a psychologist to give professional advice. I'm here to show you my mistakes and how I fixed them or coped with them to be a better person. Go out there and don't look back, you too can be better and achieve your goals and dreams. To infinity and beyond.


**PS**. If you bought this book think of it as a charity. This book is helping my son go to college.

This is book is dedicated to the three most important people in my life which I call my A.L.I. Andre, Leilani and Ian.

**A**ndre, I haven't told this to anyone but you are the reason I quit drinking. I love you with all my heart and I didn't want to be a bad role model for you, so I decided to quit drinking to be a better person you can look up to.

**L**eilani, you are the flower in my life. You gave me hope when I didn't have any. You wanted to be with me and play with me when I felt lonely and depressed. You gave me hope that one day I would have a flower that will shine a light in my life. Leilani you are my Hero.

**I**an, if it wasn't for you I would have never achieved my dreams. After you were born I decided to reach for my goals and work hard. Your birth gave me the courage and balls I needed to step up to the plate and swing for the moon. Everything I do is for you. I love you now and forever.

# How To Be A Dad Without A Dad

# ABOUT THE AUTHOR

This is where I talk about myself in the third person.

Jose was born and raised in Guatemala. He has been a proud citizen of the United States of America since 2016. He didn't have a dad growing up but had a great brother by his side. Jose has helped raise his nephews and niece and is a proud parent himself. Jose has been part of the Radio Broadcasting industry for 15 years. He has plenty of radio and broadcast experience and has been part of many popular radio shows.

His writing skills started in college where he wrote many student plays and was part of the theater department at Glendale Community College. The college produced some of his plays, and he was nominated to the KCACTF Region VIII festival in 2003 for his acting skills. When he became a father, he decided to achieve his dreams and started acting and writing again.

He had some questions on how to raise his own son and discovered that by not having a dad he didn't have a point of reference to go by and decided to put his own personal experience to help other fathers with the same issues. At the moment Jose's main focus is how to be a good role model for his son, nephews, and niece and how to provide a better future for his family.

Jose is also a tall, good-looking male Model with a full set of hair..... Main reason he started in a Great Clips national commercial.

JoseDeLaRoca.com

I would like to thank:

Andy, Jon Naudi, Raul, Enon, Mike Chocolate Timpson, Paulina, and Kenia, for all your help and support.

Follow me: @delarocajose

Instagram: @howtobeadadwithoutadad

Website: Howtobeadadwithoutadad.com

Blog: howtobeadadwithoutadad.blogspot.com

Podcast: soundcloud.com/howtobeadadwithoutadad

Copyright © 2018 by Jose De La Roca
All rights reserved. No part of this book may be reproduced, scanned,
or distributed in any printed or electronic form without permission.
First Edition: May 3rd, 2018
Printed in the United States of America

Made in the USA
San Bernardino, CA
29 June 2018